By Gary Beck

Novels

Extreme Change
Acts of Defiance
Flawed Connections
Call to Valor
Sudden Conflicts
Crumbling Ramparts
Flare Up
Raise High the Walls
Still Defiant
State of Rage
Wave Length
Protective Agency
Obsess
Still Obsessed

Poetry

Expectations
Days of Destruction
Dawn in Cities
Assault on Nature
Songs of a Clerk
Civilized Ways
Conditioned Response
Displays
Perceptions
Fault Lines
Tremors
Virtual Living
Perturbations
Blossoms of Decay
Rude Awakenings
Blunt Force
Remission of Order
Contusions
Transitions
Earth Links
Mortal Coil
Desperate Seeker
Too Harsh For Pastels
Temporal Dreams
Severance
Redemption Value
Fractional Disorder
Disruptions
Ignition Point
Learning Curve
Resonance
Turbulence
Lacerations

Play CollectionsL

The Big Match and other one act plays
Collected Plays of Gary Beck Volume I
Plays of Aristophanes translated then directed by Gary Beck
Collected Plays of Gary Beck Volume II
Four Plays of Moliere translated then directed by Gary Beck

Short Story Collections

A Glimpse of Youth
Now I Accuse and other stories

Lacerations

Gary Beck

ISBN: 978-81-8253-899-3

First Edition: 2022
Rs. 200/-

Cyberwit.net
HIG 45 Kaushambi Kunj, Kalindipuram
Allahabad - 211011 (U.P.) India
http://www.cyberwit.net
Tel: +(91) 9415091004
E-mail: info@cyberwit.net

To all the good people getting hurt

while trying to do the right thing

Poems from Lacerations have appeared in

Adelaide Literary Mag, Bewildering Stories, Bonnie's Crew, Dissident Voice, Dreich Magazine (Hybrid Press), El Portal, Journal of Expressive Writing, Mason Street, Page & Spine Pandemonium Press, Poetic Medicine, Polseguera Magazine, Scarlet Leaf Review, Scimitar Magazine (Wolfian Press), Setu Magazine, The Chicago Record, Verse of Silence, Wilderness Literary Review & Press, Winamop Magazine, WineDrunk SideWalk, Words for the Wild, Zin Daily (Zvonay Nari – Cultural Production Coop)

Contents

Pet Disposal

Many people keep pets,
dogs, cats, exotics,
and easily tire
of the maintenance,
walks, food, Vet visits,
constant demands.
Birds, the easiest pets
to get rid of.
Open the window,
dump them out,
shut the window,
watch them fly away,
neither fast, nor far,
lacking energy,
endurance
after life in a cage.
Then not finding
the food and water dish,
unable to stand the cold,
silently fold their wings,
die, unnoticed
by the passersby,
brief flutter of freedom
quickly ended.

High Abuse

I once dreamed of a land
where all were free
with equal opportunity.
Grade school cured me of that.
As I grew up
prejudice, discrimination,
hatred, violence
pervaded my country,
poisoning the home of democracy.
It took a while for me to learn
our rulers weren't elected officials,
but obscure oligarchs
who bought legislators
for their own needs,
rather then the nation.
And when amoral corporations
abandoned America
for higher profit abroad,
removing a blue collar class
that resisted the bosses,
leaving a rust belt
to defile the landscape.
And year after year
more and more of our rights
were taken away
until our birthright is tarnished
by ruthless exploiters
of a once hopeful people.

Celebrations

Consumerism
probably always existed,
desire in the cave
for meat, fat, fur
motivating some
to long hours hunting.

The Industrial Revolution
probably spawned
mass consumption,
from more goods produced
then ever before.

And the celebration
of material things
grew and grew,
yet appetites of greed
were never sated.

First newspapers,
then radio
told us what to buy
and the enchanting voices
from the wonderous boxes
reassured us we bought wisely.

Then the visual delight
of television

revealed what we'd possess
in all its splendor.

Clothing, computers, cars,
tantalizingly close,
urging us acquire
what we did
or did not need.

And those who ruled
our troubled land
encouraged us
to be condemned
for excess spending
on holidays.

While those who have
spend billions
on Halloween,
Thanksgiving,
Christmas,
the privileged festive,
the rest do without.

Teetering

I live on the edge,
not from daring,
or adventure,
but from frailty,
my body become so fragile
the tiniest slip,
the least mistake
that makes me fall
ends my life.
I have no resilience,
cannot hope to recuperate
from any damage,
lacking so many resources
recovery impossible
from a failed state.

Ghost Town

In the old west
abandoned towns
quickly decayed,
buildings rotted
from harsh winds,
abrasive elements,
until the only pedestrians
were tumbleweeds,
fleeting monuments
to human habitation.

A village, town, or city
only continues
if people endure,
have food, shelter, clothing,
other necessities
to sustain life.

When the economy collapses
diminishing opportunity
leads to departure.
Conditions deteriorate.
Subsistence is difficult.
The young flee, others,
those who are mobile
seek better surroundings.

Those who remain die off
and the human enclosure

hacked out of wilderness
crumbles and is forgotten.

As I travel through my city
of cracked sidewalks of despair,
empty stores gape at my passing,
no longer supporting people
for work, play, a home.

I see so much decay
I fear there may be
a turning point,
when the great metropolis
will begin to fade away.

Birdless

The birds have left
Afghanistan, Syria, Gaza,
many other countries,
constant explosions traumatic,
destruction of habitat
preventing nesting,
so they perished,
or moved on
until the next place
detonates,
strewing feathers everywhere,
fragile flyers
not as valued as children,
children not valued enough
to stop the wars.

Art is Short

Before portrait painting
people didn't really know
what they looked like.
The water was still clean,
so sometimes they'd get a peek,
though they didn't want to get caught looking.
Of course a friend, lover or relative
might tell them what they looked like,
but they couldn't be sure
if what they said was true.

They believed when told
the color of their eyes,
and they could feel
the shape of their nose,
but the rest was mystery.

Then the portrait painters
actually artisans,
began painting faces
on commission.
And if they made folk look
a little better than they were
that assured payment,
possible future referrals,
which might lead
to a life of comfort.

The best of these hirelings
made their subjects look handsome.

Then artisans became artists
reflecting 19th century changes,
political, social, economic,
creating a new caste,
many of them believing
they were superior
to the bourgeoisie,
the new customers
that allowed a better life
for Mom and the kids,
though they didn't understand
fine art nonsense
and the weird bohemians
with unstable lifestyles.

But many creative spirits
found out the hard way
they had to get paid to live.
And most of them lacked
transactional skills
and had a hard time
finding customers willing to pay
for less than realistic faces,
until the artists became famous.

Then avaricious collectors
bought previously despised paintings
from once scorned and mocked artists,
now illustrious possessions
on indifferent walls,
where expensive paintings
soon went unnoticed,
another artwork deleted
from a confused world.

Who Suffereth...

As we submerge
into inequality
the homeless are subtracted
from civilization,
children who committed no crime,
veterans who served their country,
exiled to the streets
in an ungiving society
that renounced morality.

Growing Darkness

They didn't teach us in grade school
about oligarchs.
We did not know
that democracy
was an illusion,
backed up with eloquent words,
exquisite documents
political deceptions.
The little I learned
abut history
indicates
we were always ruled
by the rich and powerful,
who once lived in castles
so we knew who was oppressing us.
Now the American dream
that once allowed
a better life for millions
has been subverted
and the forces of darkness,
nurtured by greed and hatred,
pervade a confused land
that desperately needs
citizens of goodwill
to guide us out of destruction.

We, the...

Politics has always been dirty
whether in our land
or another,
past, present
a revealing study
of ego, greed, corruption
in Western democracies,
convincing the people
they have opportunity,
never confessing
it's only for some,
most of us too busy
struggling for survival
for revolutionary ardor.

Gross Vulgarities

Shoppers fight for merchandise,
hurting each other
to possess goods
of limited value,
encouraged by merchants
who promote mayhem
in search of greater profits.

Spectators crassly applaud
the record price of a painting
that sells at auction
by a once despised artist,
whose work is now a trophy
in the hall of acquisitions.

Santa Con,
the lurid display
of drunken louts,
lying in the gutter
covered in vomit,
dressed in the uniform
that once symbolized
Peace on Earth,
goodwill to men,
now eroding the last traces
of illusory innocence.

Personal Revelations

I was cursed as a child
with endless torment
turning my mind and soul
out of proportion
to my earthly pain,
the only solace
blessed escape
into wondrous books
that did not cure my anguish,
but took me away
to enchanting lands
that became part of me.

Then I could only see
the evils that tortured me,
oblivious to the suffering
of those about me
a prisoner of my own pain,
only allowed escape
in stolen voyages,
the Iliad, the Odyssey,
always being Odysseus
rather than Achilles,
as I became
for blissful moments
those who I read,
briefly comforting me
in a world of hurt.

As I got a little older
I struck back at others
in blind rage, retaliation,
an oppressed response
for what I endured,
dispensing pain,
often unprovoked,
to friends and strangers.
And the evil I did
still lives within me.
Yet I found nightly escape
as I was Hamlet, not Macbeth,
D'Artagnan, not Porthos,
and for brief moments
my too, too solid flesh
dwelt in other lives.

Then destiny took a hand
shattering my young teen life
with a terrible affliction
that altered the fumbling path
I blindly followed
leading to death,
averted by dreadful illness
compelling rebirth
to permit continuation,
still trapped in suffering,
still oblivious
to the suffering of others,
I discovered poetry
Byron, Keats, Shelley,
Whitman, O Whitman,
who told me:

'Resist much. Obey little'
and I obeyed him.

Once again cast adrift
on uncertain seas
I sought sensual pleasures
fleeing the painful past,
yet began to look around
and see the suffering of others,
and within my fragile soul
a great rage was born
at the injustices I saw
everywhere I went,
yet helpless to prevent,
and plunged into the anguish
of Ahab, Tom Joad, Gene Gant,
struggling to comprehend
the iniquity of man.

I wanted to remit
the wrongs inflicted on the innocent
but knew not how
and wandered from place to place,
always seeking, but never finding
a path to redress grievances.
Bereft of math and science
I took some nourishment
from artful creations,
The Divine Comedy,
Katha Sarit Sagara,
Genji Monogatari,
tasting as much as I could
of different climes.

Although still lost
on unlit paths
to meaningful action,
made more confining
by reinventing the wheel
day after day
because I trusted no one,
not even the poets
Baudelaire, Mallarmé,
Apollinaire, Valery,
exquisite lives away
from the streets of squalor
where I lived
surrounded by the oppressed
denied the benefits
my land promised
to all.

I began to move out of myself,
used the magic of theater
to outreach to others, quickly learned
Oedipus Tyrannus, King Lear,
wasn't for everyone.
Yet I began to heal myself
with the medicine of art
and was compelled to heal others.
How good it was
to bring Moliere, Aristophanes,
other delightful comedies
to poverty populations,
underserved communities
whose lives I couldn't change,
but could briefly enrich with laughter.

I was fortunate enough
to find others who helped me
bring the beauty of theater
to the needy and deprived
who forgot their pain for an hour,
not enough to make things better,
but perhaps a glimpse of other worlds
that could be aspired to.
Yet we were despised by
the theater world
for bringing plays to public housing,
prisons, hospitals for the isolated,
while the smug theater network
ignored our productions
in our Off Off Broadway theater
of neglected and forgotten classics,
as if we didn't exist.

No one in theater ever worked harder
mentally, emotionally, physically,
or truer then I did
to create stage beauty.
And many talented people
contributed their best,
gave me their best
and I couldn't reward them
for professional efforts
that delighted small audiences,
but the doors were always shut
that prevented performance
on a bigger stage.

Despite painful failures
we created wonderful shows,
the doors of my theater closed,
resources expended,
opportunity departed
to bring plays to audiences.
I have not lost my love of theater
and mourn its passing,
as other performing arts are passing
in the age of hi-tech visuals,
Netflix far more accessible
then unknown stage ventures,
except for musicals
that will sing and dance
until heard no more live,
replaced by electronic presentations
requiring no audience commitment.

And as the traditional audiences
grey out, grow too feeble to attend
once challenging productions
now mostly bland and safe,
those who still go to the classics
given drama-lite,
tragedies made lo-cal,
turning them into dumb comic turns,
producers, directors
not trusting audiences
to share the anguish
of the Iceman, Godot,
reducing them to silly horseplay
instead of towering stature.

If anyone bothers again
to do the great tragedies
for television conditioned viewers
they will be condescending spectacles
for the audience to laugh at,
shared suffering, catharsis,
completely forgotten,
disappeared by the timid,
clasping their illusions
of serious theater
as it dwindles to obsolescence,
facilitated by presenters of pap,
whose most noted contribution
to the art of theater
is more expensive tickets,
sky-high box office prices
another donation
to the demise of theater.

I do not spend time on nostalgia
dreaming of performances past.
Yet I never forget
theater once thrilled audiences,
historically the most powerful
of the performing arts
that made people feel
as well as think.
As we grow more confined
to our various dwellings
by bigger and bigger tvs,

other electronic diversions,
our brave nation is changing

and we become passive spectators
accepting what is done to us,
losing the will to resist
the many injustices
inflicting our country.

Devaluation

Concern for the needy
was part of many societies
until demand exhausted resources,
exceeded tolerance levels
of those who might help
alleviate the suffering,
become so widespread
that even wealthy countries
abandoned the destitute,
no longer able to afford
basic services for many,
while the few feast.

Urban Cycles

For a city to be welcoming
it must have
a thriving economy
with well-paying jobs,
shops of all kinds
to provide for needs,
a cultural life
so they don't feel like serfs,
an ethos to reassure people
they are not just beasts
preying on each other.
When those elements fray
dangers emerge,
stores close, housing decays,
unemployment soars
disorder spreads like a disease
infecting all but the rich.

Forgettable

We remembered the Alamo
for a while,
as long as we were grabbing
land that wasn't ours,
but by the Civil War we forgot.

We remembered the Maine
for a while,
as long as we were grabbing
countries that weren't ours,
but by World War I we forgot.

We remembered Pearl Harbor
for a while,
as long as we conquered
an enemy empire,
but by the Vietnam War we forgot.

The Cold War changed everything.
We don't want to remember Vietnam,
9/11, Iraq, Afghanistan,
since we didn't accomplish much,
defeat our enemies.

As our empire contracts
we no longer call for crusades,
interconnected economically
with friends and foes,
unwilling to risk loss of income.

Cold Streets

Winter is early this year
usurping Fall,
bringing frigid days
prompting us to dress warm,
those who have warm coats,
the rest shiver,
unable to afford
comfort clothing,
economic constraint
denying down garments,
allowing Iphones, tv,
poverty's compensation.

Callous Neglect

In ancient Athens,
the first democratic society,
unwanted children
were exposed on mountains,
survival coincidental.

In Restoration London
unwanted children
were put on unpaved streets,
survival haphazard.

In democratic America
unwanted children
are warehoused in foster care,
sentenced to homeless shelters,
murdered by caregivers,
most of them far removed
from the benefits
of the American Dream

Sad Song

Birds, fragile creatures
always lose
conflicts with humans.
As we destroy habitat
with urbanization,
agriculture, fracking,
endless assaults
on a vulnerable land,
whose owners don't care
if there are fewer birds,
concerned with their power,
not unenforceable rights
of other species.

New York City

Settled earlier
then many American cities,
but not so old
as most in Europe,
yet somehow became
the greatest builder
erecting more skyscrapers
than the rest of the world,
pioneering public housing
infrastructure like no other,
the urban capitol
of entertainment, vice,
with immense riches,
yet a poverty population
that shames democracy,
a complex union
of the good and bad,
a tantalizing mixture
of beauty, ugliness.

Tempo

The rush hour routine
sets millions in motion
going to jobs that pay the bills,
support industry and commerce,
keep the city running
as long as there's power,
transportation, food,
the needs we might still control,
as we neglect potable water,
breathable air.

Last Glance

I watch the decay
of the promised land,
frail institutions
no longer protecting the people,
as the few consume
as if there's no tomorrow,
hastening a poor tomorrow,
and I can only wonder
if someone watched
in ancient Rome
as the barbarian tide
engulfed the empire.

Frenemy

Sometimes weather is a friend,
sometimes it's an enemy.
When we need rain for crops
and it rains helpfully
our lives are bettered.
But when it rains, rains, rains,
floods devastate our land
destroying property, lives.
The variety of climate change
brings bigger storms,
longer droughts, dangerous changes,
that protected city dwellers
are frequently sheltered from,
grown oblivious
to the perils of nature.

Where Am I

When I was young
I did not speculate
as some friends did
of an alternate universe,
always better than ours,
without war, disease,
famine, poverty, greed.
Utopia was unimaginable.
One friend always rambled on
of suddenly waking up
in another, better Earth.
I never laughed at him.
After all, some of my ideas
about social justice,
equal opportunity,
seemed just as alien to him.
Then Trump was elected.
I worried about our republic
when so many voted for him.
Then he started breaking down
the pillars of democracy,
removing the protection of the people,
health, income, security.
Yet after all he did
to harm the present and future,
people still like him,
making me wonder
is it mass hypnosis, psychosis,
or an alternate Earth.

Fragile Life

Butterflies need forests,
open areas in the woods,
grass, bushes, trees
to go about butterfly business.
When concrete prevails
nourishment departs
and we are deprived
of elegant flutterers
giving moments of beauty,
easily forgotten.

Consuming Streets

Midtown Manhattan
once a hub of prosperity,
now each corner
ravaged by empty stores,
festooned with the homeless,
one tale after another
on cardboard signs
of desperation,
abandoned citizens fear
there is no salvation,
as they slowly dissolve
on indifferent sidewalks.

Theft

Parks are designed so people
can have a taste of greenery
in the concrete wilderness.
Somehow in America
the lowest elements
of a confused society,
junkies, dealers, muggers,
denizens of viceland,
move into the parks
dispensing pollution,
until decent citizens
have few options
but grassless places.

Afghanistan

A strife-torn land
ravaged by invaders
time and time again
eager for conquest
to further empire,
sooner or later
each defeated
by unruly tribesman,
harsh environment
no comfort for the enemy.
A sufficiency
of blood and treason,
lack of victory
defeated invaders
who returned home
humbled
by a primitive people,
leaving no mementos
on a rugged landscape
unwelcoming to locals
and foreigner alike,
until the hi-tech age
when intruders linger
with mighty machines
that are still defeated
by intractable tribesmen.

Distressed

Apprehension in a fearsome world,
some go through day to day interactions
with incrementing dread, enhanced
by anticipation of devastating storms,
fretting increasing violence,
dangers once imagined, now real,
combining for constant discomfort,
that which might happen
too disturbing to be ignored.

Chill, City

Cold winds begin to blow.
People course the streets faster,
urgent to escape the chill.
The grey sky darkens.
Snow begins to fall.
A pure white coat caresses the city.
People frolic in the snow,
bring out skis, snowshoes, sleds,
make snowmen, snow angels,
enjoy the respite from concrete.
Then the snowfall ends.
The day gets warmer.
City soot prevails.
The snow turns black from urban grime.
The brief vacation is over.
People trudge about more wearily
hoping to endure 'til spring.

Moral Decay

A normal day
in the wealthy city,
people go to work,
those with jobs.
The anger quotient
seethes at its usual level,
fights and murders
an urban constant.
And children go to school,
more then a million of them,
with many parents hoping
for a better future.
Yet 10% of New York City schoolchildren
are homeless,
a disgrace and tragedy.
While at the same time
Americans
spent 9 billion dollars
on Halloween,
though we couldn't afford
to save the children.

Unempowered

The 41st President
unfortunately may have been
the last qualified president
to encompass the demands of office.
Successors have had little
of his experience
to be the leading citizen
of a troubled nation
in need of democracy,
not allowed by the oligarchs.

Electronic Purchasing

Rural folk
used to look different
than city folk
who spent more on clothes,
more aware of style,
until the information age
when internet technology
made it easier
to shop at home,
harsh weather,
dangerous streets
prime motivation
to buy online.

Doctor Visit

The ill line up and wait
hoping for treatment, cure.
Officious clerks ignore you
as you stand on frail legs,
unsure if you might fall
before you're called.
You're sent to a waiting room
and wait. And wait.
Then, name mispronounced
you're taken to an examination room,
where you wait. And wait. And…
A nurse comes in,
takes vitals, says:
"The doctor will be right with you."
You wait. And wait. And…
It is almost an hour
after your appointment time.
The doctor comes in,
tells you to do things at home,
tells you to come back in three months
and quickly departs
without giving you a chance
to discuss your condition.
You go back to the desk,
wait with others
to make an appointment.

Advanced Confinement

Internet technology
allows low cost connection,
a transformative role
changing the economics
of communication.

Artificial Intelligence technology
allows low cost discovery,
using the vast amounts of data,
the resource of the digital age,
to make predictions.

As we are encouraged
more and more to stay at home,
electronic outreach
will bring everything we need
without our leaving the house.

Moderates

When it's not too hot
and not too cold
urban residents
enjoy themselves more
than in extreme weather,
conditioned to indoors
spending most of their time
with climate controlled tv,
or the internet,
not as hardy
as their forebearers.

Debate

Over the years
many have argued
whether or not
there is dignity in labor.
If one toils mightily
yet gets no fame,
fortune, other reward
except subsistence,
some believe
we are just slightly evolved
from the beasts.
If we are part
of the great mass
of undistinguished humanity
living obscurely
by the sweat of effort,
many more feel
it is insufficient
to justify the purpose
of our species' existence.

Growth Spurt

In 1814
we weren't more advanced
then in 1714.
But in 1914
we were industrialized
and made modern wars
with tanks, airplanes,
powerful weapons
to kill each other.
By 2014
we progressed enough
to destroy the planet,
leading some to speculate
that by 2114
we could obliterate
the solar system.

Faker Spouts

The President complains
about fake news
as if he invented the concept
used by so many before him
and frightened followers believe him,
as he leads them to confusion
hopefully not persuading them
to drink Kool-Aid.

Death Calls

Living creatures
are disappearing
faster and faster.
Feeble efforts
to save some species
inadequate,
elimination
easier
then conservation.

Appraisal

I have a rendezvous with death,
tryst, encounter, assignation
that I am not eager to attend,
but will comply when I must,
however reluctant, preferring
to linger as long as I can
in this exhilarating life
as long as my mind is clear.
Otherwise I'm another drain
on finite resources
consuming, but not contributing,
of minimal redeeming value
better dispensed with
that others may subsist.

Pollution

It is difficult to understand
why representatives of the people
allow dumping of toxic waste
in our vulnerable waterways
at a time when water
is a diminishing resource
in a thirsty world
that cannot do without
the precious fluid.

Seduction

So many ways
to tempt us,
take from us
what often shouldn't be given.
Money, power, sex,
so many ways
to lead us into concession
until we are conditioned
to yield more than we should,
whether to abusive leaders,
anonymous corporations,
corrosive relationships.
Those of us
too weak to resist
seductive offerings
are sometimes captives
of unrequited desire.

Park Pleasures

Music echoes through Bryant Park.
People hum and sway to the tunes.
Others enjoy themselves,
tourists and locals
on a warm, summer day.
But nearby, on unheard streets,
the rejected homeless
submerge into the pavements.

Dangerous Time

I used to fear
that incrementally
democracy was ebbing away.
Now it's rushing away
and the shades of oligarchy
are crushing the people
with terrible burdens
we may not recover from,
a perilous crisis
without leaders to save us.

Change

It's still mid-August
in a temperate clime,
but it was so cool
early this morning
that I wore long underwear,
reminding me
summer is over.

Moving On

Bryant Park is so busy
that certain birds moved out,
unable to compete
with pushy pigeons,
aggressive sparrows.
So birds I once saw,
vireo, catbird, thrush,
lots of migrators twice a year,
no longer appear to please the eye
and nobody else believes
they're entitled to space.

The March of History

We are unprepared
for serious disaster
bio, chemical, nuclear attack.
The loss of power,
death and destruction
sufficient to end
the brief reign
of the American Empire
of economic conquest,
ephemeral endurance.
When we can't recover
from a severe hurricane
some of us conclude
there's no way to survive
national collapse.

Seasonal Shift

Summer is almost over.
The hot sun begins to move away
and a pre-chill creeps into my bones,
reminding me to take out sweaters,
put on more garments to stay warm,
expectation of another summer
uncertain.

Danger Zone

City people
grow lax and casual
provided with amenities
to get from place to place
and frequently don't notice
hazards of the streets,
cracks, potholes, construction,
red light jumpers,
many tuned out
listening to IPODS,
many texting,
all at imminent risk
from unexpected dangers.

Perceptions

In 1980
Bryant Park was a cesspool
of illegal drugs,
junkies, dealers, muggers,
prostitutes, criminals,
concealed from the public
behind tall bushes
surrounding the park.
Only the unwary entered.
But if you time traveled
to 2018
you'd find a neat pocket jewel
that pleases all users
and you'd never know
the woes besetting the people,
the erosion of democracy,
the declining middle class,
the disappearance of jobs,
a growing poverty population,
on a warm, spring day
in Bryant Park.

Adaption

The temperature is almost 100F.
Some people are sniveling,
complain bitterly about the heat.
But it's not the Sahara
and for one day, city folk
could stop griping.
Oases are everywhere.
Water is plentiful
and the odds are probable
that few will die
from one hot day.

Activism

All the protests we believe in
meant to improve the system
rarely change things for the better,
just allow us a means of complaint
as we passionately object
to a succession of abuses
by the lords of profit,
who do not care
about the rest of us.

Continuation

The last week of summer,
hot, hazy, still full of life.
The birds are singing.
They may or may not know
winter is coming
and many will not see spring.
Soon the land will go to sleep
with no guarantee
it will wake up again,
just the thoughtless assumption
that life continues
despite the ravages of man.

Oglescope

The weather is still warm enough
for women to wear short skirts,
tight tops, bare midriffs,
a visual pleasure
for those who care to look,
soon to be removed
with the first chill of fall.

Forecast Dim

Seasonal change
affects people
in different ways.
Some move a little faster
eager to escape
the coming cold.
Others plod along
resigned to discomfort,
as if Nature targets them.
Small farmers worry
more than anyone,
since bad weather
ruins crops.
City people complain
more than most,
except when snow
transforms everything
into a winter wonderland.

Alteration

People sit in Bryant Park
enjoying the safe hint of nature,
lots of flowers, aging sycamore trees.
Game areas, food stands, diversions,
all combine for a pleasant experience.
No one able to imagine
this oasis in the city
was once a pollution site
of drugs, crime and violence,
strenuously avoided
by tourists and locals alike.

Season's End

Summer is ended.
The last days of warmth
drift into the distance.
Basking in sunshine
already forgotten,
apprehensive of winter
bringing obligatory chills.

Decay of Democracy

The political charade
in divided America
becomes tenser daily
as issues, agendas, ambitions
rasp the public well-being
trying to survive
an irresponsible President,
who tells the people
'there are good people
on each side'
when nazis and radicals
fight each other
for extremist views,
instead of stopping them.

Summons For Life

Unnatural deposits
of toxic material
undegradable,
plastics strangling the ocean,
waste of every kind
polluting the air, earth,
leaders too ignorant
to recognize the danger
on a fragile planet
that sustains life.
Miracle? Coincidence?
As we need a wake-up call
to preserve the future.

Population Density

When I was young
I traveled many roads
in my land, foreign lands,
all different,
some close to nature.
Now I've become citified
confined to concrete,
familiar with subways,
not where forests grow.
Trapped in urban maze
in a land grown foreign
I no longer know
where I belong.

Shadow Rule

America is divided
the media proclaims,
a democratic illusion
purporting two sides,
however extreme
deluding us we have choices,
while the oligarchs
fund who they will,
however unqualified
to rule a nation.

The Land of Confusion

A major hurricane
is coming to Florida.
Experts say the worst
in a hundred years.
While our president jokes
with rabid supporters
far away, dry and safe.
A better person
would go near the scene,
rally help, not votes,
too dumb to know
disaster is more important
then partisan politics.
But he's what we have
and the scariest thing
is how many Americans
think he's doing well.

Capital Gains

The stock market goes up and down.
Investors cheer when it goes up.
Investors moan when it goes down.
Profit, loss the only concerns.
Meanwhile millions of Americans
suffer devastating loss
from disastrous storms
that ravaged large sections
of an already damaged land,
while greedy corporations,
swollen with tax breaks
at the expense of the people,
would never consider
donations to the needy
desperate for assistance.

Con Artists

Corporations,
a clever invention
designed to protect
the wealth of participants
from consequences
of failure, greed, stupidity
with limited liability
to allow escape
from economic errors,
since corporate existence
has become so normal
we no longer question
that they exploit the public.

Dead End Road

Potholes in my mind
trip up my memory,
disremembering
persons, places, names, dates,
accumulated knowledge
that once made me
a functional being.

Glum Picture

Wherever I go
the people of my land
do not look happy.
Fortunately,
not all of them,
but so many,
I did not know
misery possessed so many.
Even mothers with children
do not look glad,
at least while outside,
making me fear
for the well-being of the nation.

Ponderous Changes

In the 1830's
Americans went west
for free land,
an independent life
without government,
other restrictions.
And they endured
different conditions,
drought, floods, hostile indians
whose land was stolen.
All for the sake of freedom.
In the 1930's
life in America had changed
and more and more people
lived in towns and cities,
easier for government to control.
For a brief while the workers
had some hope to resist the bosses
who controlled the wealth,
the means of production.
But all too soon
the children of the union leaders
joined the children of the bosses
in identical comforts,
ending resistance to oligarchy.

Sickness

Across my country
the ill, sick, ailing, diseased
flock to doctors, clinics,
hospitals
hoping for a cure
of whatever plagues them
many treatable
except old age,
terminal disease
withdrawal from struggle.

Park Change

Summer ends at Bryant Park.
The ice skating rink opens.
Small vendor stalls fill the walkways.
The recreation moves indoors,
or departs until Spring.
The usage of the park
is almost always positive,
an encouraging change
in a careless city
that often surrenders its parks
to the lowest social elements
blighting the urban oasis.

Land of the Free

The land of the free
is bitterly divided
and reason has departed
from the warring parties,
no longer willing
to compromise,
so the wealthy do
as they always do,
still allowing some of us
the democratic illusion
of choosing our government,
while many of us
don't realize the oligarchs
select our representatives,
obliging them
to serve their masters.

High Crimes

Homeless children suffer
more then other children
from lack of identity,
cast adrift
in an uncaring land
no fault of their own,
opportunity removed
despite the constitutional
guarantees of l, l,
the pursuit of h,
obliterated,
as we do less and less
for innocent victims.

A Mighty Oath

When I was in grade school
I pledged allegiance
to the flag
of one country,
indivisible,
with liberty and justice…
You know the rest.
It didn't seem to work for me,
but I didn't know if it worked for others.
Now that I am old
I still pledge allegiance
despite divisiveness,
liberty fraying for many,
justice for few,
but until things get worse
we're still better than most.

Beleaguered

A warm November day.
People pack away their parkas,
scarves, heavy sweaters,
for a rare treat
comfortable and casual.
Yet while many are indulging
in the pleasant sunshine
messengers of hate,
domestic and foreign
attack our citizens,
some with phobic claims,
others unleashing insanity
on a beleaguered land
that has forgotten
how to heal its wounds.

Public Shame

New York City admits
10% of its grade school children
are homeless.
10%.
Yet there is no public outcry,
no calls for crusade,
no demonstrations,
just an agonizing silence
while tens of thousands
of innocent children,
who committed no crime
are cast off
as if worthless,
in a confused society
that has forgotten
children come before
most of the issues
tormenting our land.

Eyeful

The thongs of summer
are now concealed
like other revealing garments
recently displaying
alluring flesh
that tempted, provoked,
interest in shapely bodies,
while women realize
the colder it gets
the more they must cover.

Vestiges

When we are in our pleasure
we never notice
the suffering of others,
too preoccupied
with ephemeral distractions
to recognize
fragile entitlements.
And when the delights of the city
go up in flames,
crumble into dust,
covered in tidal surge
there will be lamentations
not for what they could have done
to allay the suffering of others,
but for lost comforts
that proved fleeting.

Painful Change

The leaves are falling.
So are people's faces,
woefully accepting
summer is over.
The elderly timidly
walk icy streets
fearful they may not see
another season.
Grey skies affect everything
in the dreary city,
thoughts of warmth
now forgotten,
unless Spring comes again.

Removed

Only the homeless
lack tv, the internet
and cannot connect
to humanity,
consigned to squalid shelters,
abandoned on ravenous streets
that devour the unprotected,
this harsh life
does not cherish
the non prosperous.

Imperiled State

A balmy fall day
right after elections.
We walk confusing streets
many without heavy coats
yet I do not know
how many are concerned
with the future of the republic.

The media entertains us
with election results
creating drama
for interested customers.
And all the while
there is fervent belief
that Democrats
are different then Republicans,
since so many do not know
the same people pay both sides,
ensuring services
for anonymous masters.

Rejects

Children of despair
populate my land
increasing in numbers annually,
a criminal dividend
wasting youth, resources, the future
as an indifferent system
that does not care
who survives, flourishes,
those who could help
completely preoccupied
with profit and loss,
continuation of the disadvantaged
of no concern.

Urban Woe

A great city
is known for many things,
some in the tourist guides,
restaurant guides,
entertainment guides,
and the middle class
still lives well,
those who have not been attrited
by loss of jobs,
other income shattering occurrences.
While the working class
and the poverty class
slowly submerge
into struggles for survival.
The homeless sit on many corners
cardboard signs proclaiming need,
mostly ignored,
too many demands
in a time of decline,
while most of the people
dwell in comfort,
immune to deprivation.

Cold Front

Winter winds blow harshly
as people trudge unkind streets
heads lowered, backs bent,
walking an exertion
especially for the elderly,
aged bodies stiffening in the cold,
urgently intent
on reaching somewhere warm.

End of Term

A President dies.
Some mourn genuinely.
Some pay lip service.
Most go about their business
as if nothing happened
that affected them.
Too many of us don't realize
that although he is a figurehead
created by special interests,
some are more effective than others
in serving the nation.

Variant

A warm day in December
startles the city dwellers
out of winter wear
for brief enjoyment
of the daily routine
without heavy clothing.

www.ingramcontent.com/pod-product-compliance
Lightning Source LLC
LaVergne TN
LVHW091606170726
843492LV00007B/2292

* 9 7 8 8 1 8 2 5 3 8 9 9 3 *